Test Your Verbs

Jake Allsop

PENGUIN ENGLISH

For Jenny

Pearson Education Limited
Edinburgh Gate
Harlow
Essex CM20 2JE, England
and Associated Companies throughout the world.

ISBN-10: 0-582-45176-0
ISBN-13: 978-0-582-45176-6
Fourth impression 2006

First published 2002
Text copyright © Jake Allsop 2002

Designed and typeset by Pantek Arts Ltd, Maidstone, Kent
Test Your format devised by Peter Watcyn-Jones
Illustrations by Peter Standley
Printed in China   SWTC/04

Published by Pearson Education Limited in association with Penguin Books Ltd, both companies being subsidiaries of Pearson plc.

Acknowledgements
It is not customary to acknowledge one's editors: after all, they are only doing their job like the rest of us. But, in this case, my editor Fiona Davis deserves a mention. A lot of what is good in this book is the result of her patient and persistent efforts to point her author in a better direction. The blemishes that remain are mine.

For a complete list of the titles available from Penguin English please visit our website at www.penguinenglish.com, or write to your local Pearson Education office or to: Marketing Department, Penguin Longman Publishing, Edinburgh Gate, Harlow, Essex CM20 2JE.

Contents

To the student   v

Section 1: Tenses 1

1   Present simple or present continuous? 1   2

2   Present simple or present continuous? 2   4

3   What's the difference? 1   6

4   Past simple or past continuous?   7

5   Past or perfect? 1   8

6   Past or perfect? 2   10

7   Very irregular rhymes   11

8   Narrative tenses 1   12

9   Narrative tenses 2   14

10   Future tenses 1   15

11   Future tenses 2   16

Section 2: Auxiliary verbs

12   Questions and negatives   19

13   Combinations   20

14   Question tags 1   21

15   Question tags 2   22

16   Joke time   24

17   Crazy captions 1   26

Section 3: Tenses 2

18   Conditionals   28

19   Conditionals in action   29

20   Reporting direct questions   30

21   Reporting verbs   32

22   What's the difference? 2   34

Section 4: Passives

23   Passive forms   36

24   What does it mean?   37

25   Active or passive?   38

26   What needs doing?   40

27   Have something done   42

Section 5: Modal verbs

28   *Should* or *shouldn't*?   44

29   *Can, could* or *be able to*?   46

30   Modal verbs of deduction   47

31   *Have to*   48

32   *Must* or *have to*?   49

33   Crazy captions 2   50

Section 6: Verb phrases

34   Phrasal verbs 1   52

35   Phrasal verbs 2   53

36   Three-word verbs   54

37   Verbs with following preposition 1   55

38   Verbs with following preposition 2   56

Section 7: Verb patterns

39 Verb patterns 1   58

40 Verb patterns 2   59

41 Crazy captions 3   60

42 Verb patterns crossword   62

Section 8: Word building

43 Verbs beginning with
em- or en-   65

44 Word building   66

45 Verbs from adjectives
and nouns   68

46 Verb families 1   70

47 Verb families 2   71

48 Common verb prefixes 1   72

49 Prefix crossword   74

50 Common verb prefixes 2   76

Section 9: Choosing the right verb

51 Make or do?   78

52 *Say*, *speak*, *talk* or *tell*?   80

53 Expressions with *take*
or *have*   82

54 Confusing verbs   84

55 Confusing pairs   86

56 Crazy captions 4   88

57 Verb and noun   90

58 Verb and adjective   92

59 Almost an alphabet!   93

60 Idioms   94

Answers   95

To the student

According to the dictionary, verbs are 'words that signify an action, experience, occurrence or state', e.g. action: *You **are reading***; experience: *I **love** you*; occurrence: *The doorbell **rang** once*; state: *This omelette **tastes** funny*.

The English verb is deceptively simple: just four forms: *talk*, *talks*, *talking*, *talked*. Even the two hundred or so irregular verbs (mostly the most common verbs in the language), have no more than five, as in *go*, *goes*, *going*, *went*, *gone*. Compare this with the Romance languages like French or Spanish, which can have up to sixty different forms! Does this mean that English is easier than, say, Spanish? Or that you cannot express in English all the things you can express in Spanish?

Of course not! With those four or five basic forms, we use verbs like *have* and *be* (auxiliaries) and verbs like *will*, *shall*, *must*, *may*, *should* (modals) to express a wide variety of meanings, e.g. actions in progress: *it **is raining***; present result of an action begun in the past: ***Have you been waiting** long?*; time relation of two past actions: *I **opened** the letter which **had arrived** that morning*; future events and our attitude to them: *Look out, you**'re going to** fall! The plane **will be landing** at Heathrow shortly* and so on.

The sixty tests in the nine sections in this book will test your knowledge of

- the form and uses of verb tenses
- the form and uses of modal verbs
- verb collocations, e.g. *take place*, *jump to conclusions*
- word building, e.g. *simple*, *simplify*; *strong*, *strengthen*
- verb phrases, including phrasal verbs, e.g. *take off*
- gerund, participles and infinitives
- common problems, e.g. use of *make* and *do*; *say*, *tell* and *speak*

Each section begins with a short explanation of the points being tested, and many tests also have tips (advice) on how to do the test and what to look out for. Do read these explanations and tips: they are there to help you. To make the book more challenging and more fun, many different kinds of tests are used, including sentence transformation, gap-filling, crosswords, jokes, limericks and cartoons. There is a key at the back of the book so that you can check your answers. In the case of questions which are open-ended, we have given you suggested answers.

English, like any language, is designed to express many shades of meaning. One way to improve your understanding is to collect examples of verb forms in use. For example, a boy comes home from school, and his mother asks him *What **did you do** today?* while his father asks *What **have you done** today?* What can you learn about the parents' attitude from their differing questions? Look for examples which illustrate the use of particular tenses, e.g. *Prices **have gone** up a lot in the last three years* and *Prices **have been going** up steadily over the last few years*, or the use of particular verbs, e.g. *Why are you **lying** on the ground*? (stretched out) and *Why are you **lying** to me*? (not telling the truth).

We hope this book will help you strengthen your knowledge, understanding and use of verbs in English. Enjoy yourself!

Jake Allsop

Section 1: Tenses 1

CONTINUOUS TENSES

Continuous tenses are made with a form of *be + … ing*, e.g. *is doing, was doing, will be doing*. They are most often used to refer to an action which is incomplete or ongoing.
What are you doing up there on the roof?
I am learning to play the guitar.
We are holding a meeting next Saturday.
It was the rush hour and people were hurrying home from work.
The plane will be landing shortly at London Heathrow.

SIMPLE TENSES

Use the present simple:
● for permanent states or facts
This bottle holds 3 litres. Birds fly.
● for regular repeated events, including scheduled events in the future
I go to aerobics class once a week. The school years starts on 17 September.
Use the past simple:
● for completed or repeated past actions
We grew up in the country. We walked to school every day.

PERFECT TENSES

Perfect tenses are made with a form of *have* followed by the past participle, e.g. *have done, having done, had done*. They refer to an action which took place at sometime before now (present perfect), before a specified event in the past (past perfect) or before a specified point in the future (future perfect).
Have you lived here all
your life?
Where's your homework?
I haven't done it.
I have been waiting for
three hours.
I carefully opened the
parcel that my parents
had sent me.
I will have finished this
work by the time my
partner gets home.

'Have you lived here all your life?'

1 Present simple or present continuous? 1

balance	cure	~~deliver~~	eat	give	grow
keep	play	~~ride~~	sell	stand	sweep

A Say what the people in the pictures are doing. Use the verbs in the box to help you.

1

What is the postman doing?

He *is riding his bicycle backwards* .

2

What are the soldiers doing?

They _____

_____ .

3

What are the doctors doing?

They _____

_____ .

4

What is the roadsweeper doing?

He _____

_____ .

5

6

What is the gardener doing?

She _____

_____ .

What is the butcher doing?

He _____

_____ .

B Now say what the same people do for a living. Use the verbs in the box to help you.

1 What do postmen do?

They _____*deliver letters*_____ .

2 What do soldiers do?

They _____ .

3 What do doctors do?

They _____ .

4 What do roadsweepers do?

They _____ .

5 What do gardeners do?

They _____ .

6 What do butchers do?

They _____ .

Use the present continuous for an action in progress before and after the moment of speaking.

2 Present simple or present continuous? 2

Choose between the simple form and the continuous form to complete these pairs of sentences.

1 think

   a What _are you thinking_ ?

   b I _____*think*_____ I am a genius, but my dad just thinks I'm crazy!

2 expect

   a I must stay in because _____ a parcel.

   b I _____ you are tired after your walk. Come and sit down!

3 see

   a I _____ that the price of petrol has gone up 35% in the last year.

   b Dad's cough is getting worse, so he _____ a doctor this afternoon.

4 taste

   a This ice-cream _____ of garlic. I asked for chocolate flavour!

   b What are you doing?

      I _____ this cake to see if it's cooked properly.

5 have

a _____ you _____ a good time?

No, I want to go home now.

b _____ you _____ any money left?

No, I've spent it all.

---

6 depend

a Don't let me down. I _____ on you!

b Do you love me?

It _____ what you mean by 'love'.

---

7 imagine

a I _____ you must be tired after your long journey, Signor Polo.

b There aren't any ghosts in here! You _____ things.

---

8 weigh

a What are you doing?

I _____ myself.

b How much _____ you _____ ?

I don't know, I can't see the scales!

The verbs in this test have two different meanings, depending on whether the verb is used in the simple or continuous form. For example, *think* (meaning to have an opinion) is not usually used in the continuous form. If used in the continuous form, it refers to the action of thinking, e.g. *You seem very quiet. What **are** you **thinking** about*?

3 What's the difference? 1

Match the sentences with the pictures.

a	The students stood up when the teacher came into the room.
b	The students were standing up when the teacher came into the room.
c	'What do you do?' 'I work in an office.'
d	'What are you doing?' 'I'm writing a letter.'
e	It rained this morning.
f	It's been raining all morning.

Use the present perfect continuous for an action started earlier which is still going on, e.g. *I have been waiting* here since seven o'clock or for a recent action where the results can still be seen, e.g. *You are wet through! You've been swimming* in the river again, haven't you?

4 Past simple or past continuous?

Complete the story, using the verb in brackets either in the past simple or the past continuous tense.

This is a story about something that happened on board a cruise ship. The cruise ship **(1)** __was going__ (go) from London to New York. A magician on board the cruise ship **(2)** _____ (do) magic tricks to entertain the passengers. He **(3)** _____ (have) a lot of very good tricks, and **(4)** _____ (be) able to make things disappear and reappear in a really mystifying way.

Unfortunately for him, there was a parrot in the audience who kept giving the game away. The parrot **(5)** _____ (shout) things like 'It's up his sleeve!' or 'He put it in his pocket!' or 'It's in his other hand!' and in this way the parrot **(6)** _____ (manage) to spoil all the magician's tricks.

One day, the magician **(7)** _____ (perform) his show as usual. The ship was in a particularly dangerous part of the sea where there are icebergs. Suddenly, just as the magician **(8)** _____ (wave) his magic wand, the ship hit an iceberg and **(9)** _____ (sink) immediately.

The magician **(10)** _____ (find) a lifebelt, and **(11)** _____ (float) in the sea when the parrot **(12)** _____ (fly) up and landed on his lifebelt. The parrot and the magician **(13)** _____ (look) at each other for a while in silence, then the parrot **(14)** _____ (say):

'OK, I give up. What **(15)** _____ you _____(do) with the ship?'

Use the past continuous

- to show that one action was going on when another action occurred, e.g. *Unfortunately I **was looking** the other way when Beckham scored the winning goal.*
- to provide background description in a narrative, e.g. *The crowd **was going** mad with excitement, people **were throwing** their hats in the air.*

5 Past or perfect? 1

Choose between the two forms of the verb to complete the story.

This is the story of a friend of mine called Harry. Harry is a postman, and years ago he **(1) lived / ~~has lived~~** in a small bedsit. The man who **(2) rented / has rented** the flat upstairs was a police officer named Charlie. Harry used to go to bed early because he **(3) has had / had to** be up early in the morning. Unfortunately, every evening Charlie **(4) would come / has come** home, take off his boots and drop them heavily on the floor. And every evening the noise of his boots hitting the floor would wake Harry in the room below.

So, one night Harry waited up for Charlie and stopped him on the stairs.

'Good evening. I wonder if I could have a word with you.'

Charlie looked at Harry.

'I'm sorry, but do I know you? I **(5) never saw / have never seen** you before.'

'I live in this flat, directly below yours.'

'Oh, OK. Well, what can I do for you?' Charlie asked.

'I don't want to complain, but I **(6) didn't have / haven't had** a good night's sleep in months.'

'What has that got to do with me?' asked the police officer.

'Well, it's your boots. Every night for the last few months, you **(7) have come / came** home and dropped your boots on the floor and the noise wakes me up.'

'Oh, sorry about that,' said Charlie. 'I **(8) haven't done / didn't do** it on purpose. I will put them down quietly in future, I promise.'

The next night Harry **(9) went / has gone** to bed early as usual and **(10) has just fallen / had just fallen** asleep when Charlie the policeman **(11) came / has come** home. Charlie sat down on his bed, took off his right boot and dropped it heavily on the floor. Suddenly, he **(12) remembered / has remembered** his conversation with Harry.

'Oh dear!' he thought. 'I still haven't got out of the habit of throwing my boots on the floor!'

He then **(13) has taken / took** off his other boot and put it on the floor very gently without making a sound.

The following evening Harry again **(14) waited / has waited** on the stairs for Charlie.

'Goodness!' said Charlie. 'You look terrible! **(15) Didn't you sleep / Haven't you slept** last night?'

'No, I **(16) didn't / haven't**,' said Harry. 'I spent the whole night wide awake, waiting for the other boot to drop!'

Use the present perfect
- for a past action where the point of time is not definite. Compare: *I've done a lot of work lately* (indefinite) with *I did a lot of work last month* (definite).
- for an action which began in the past and has continued until the present and will possibly continue into the future, e.g. *I've lived here for three days*.

6 Past or perfect? 2

Complete the story using the forms of the verbs in the box to help you.

assured	have been listening	have both been misled
have ever even seen	~~have seen~~	heard	looked at
looked it up	phoned	went on

Two men were standing at a bus stop arguing about the spelling of a word.

'It is spelt a-t-i-s-h-o-o,' said the first.

'I (1) __*have seen*__ it written down, and I can assure you that it is spelled a-t-i-s-s-o-o,' said the second.

'I am sorry to contradict you,' said the first, 'but I (2) _____ in the dictionary last night, and it is spelt a-t-i-s-h-o-o.'

'Then I suggest you throw your dictionary away, my friend! I (3) _____ my friend last night, and he (4) _____ me that it is spelt a-t-i-s-s-o-o!'

And so it (5) _____ .

Finally a lady who was standing nearby coughed politely.

'Gentlemen, forgive me. I (6) _____ to your argument, and I am afraid you (7) _____ . The spelling is t-i-s-s-u-e.'

The two men (8) _____ her in amazement. Finally one of them said:

'I doubt if you (9) _____ a yeti, let alone (10) _____ one sneeze!'

The present perfect is also used to talk about a past action with the focus on the result of that action in the present, e.g. *Look! The dog **has chewed** my slippers!*

7 Very irregular rhymes

Complete the limericks using the verbs in brackets in the correct form. All of the verbs are irregular.

There once was a young boy from Looe
Who **(1)** _dreamt_ (dream) he had **(2)** _____ (eat) his shoe.
He **(3)** _____ (wake up) in the night
With a terrible fright
And **(4)** _____ (find) it was perfectly true!

There was a young person named Frank
Who was keen to manoeuvre a tank,
But when **(5)** _____ (give) the chance
He **(6)** _____ (make) directly for France
And **(7)** _____ (go) rather too far, so he **(8)** _____ (sink).

There was an old man of Darjeeling
Who **(9)** _____ (hang) by his feet from the ceiling.
He **(10)** _____ (fall) on his head
But **(11)** _____ (feel) nothing, he **(12)** _____ (say),
For he'd **(13)** _____ (lose) all sensation and feeling.

A fellow named Arthur McNares
(14) _____ (keep) a number of very big bears.
They **(15)** _____ (eat) so much honey
He **(16)** _____ (run) out of money
So then they **(17)** _____ (eat) Arthur – who cares?

These poems are examples of *limericks*. A *limerick* is a rhyming poem with five lines.

8 Narrative tenses 1

Put the verbs in brackets into a suitable form. In some cases, more than one form will fit.

A man lived outside London, and every day he **(1)** _travelled_ (travel) into the city to work in an office. Every morning he left home at eight o'clock, and every afternoon he came home at six o'clock. When he **(2)** _____ (arrive) home, he had a cup of coffee and told his wife what he **(3)** _____ (do) at work, and how tired he was. Then he would say to her: 'What did you do? I suppose you just stayed at home as usual?' And every day she **(4)** _____ (just / smile).

One day the man came home from work and **(5)** _____ (can) not believe his eyes: the children **(6)** _____ (still / wear) their pyjamas. They **(7)** _____ (sit) on the step, and they were really dirty.

'What **(8)** _____ (happen) to you?' he asked.

They smiled happily and said:

'We **(9)** _____ (have) so much fun today, we played in the garden, and we both **(10)** _____ (fall) in the pond!'

He noticed that their pyjamas **(11)** _____ (cover) with mud. He **(12)** _____ (not / reply) but went into the house. He looked round and saw empty food boxes everywhere, the fridge door **(13)** _____ (leave) open, and the dishes **(14)** _____ (not / do).

He then went into the living room. The TV **(15)** _____ (be) on but nobody **(16)** _____ (watch) it, and there were still marks on the carpet where he **(17)** _____ (spill) his coffee the night before.

Strangest of all, there was no sign of his wife. He wondered where on earth she had got to. He went upstairs into the bedroom and was astonished to see his wife in bed. She was still in her pyjamas and **(18)** _____ (read) a magazine.

'Are you all right?' he asked.

'Yes, dear,' she replied.

'The house looks a mess! What on earth happened here today?'

She looked at him calmly and smiled.

'You know how every day when you **(19)** _____ (come) home from work you ask me what I did today?'

'Yes, what of it?' he replied. 'What are you getting at?'

'Well, today, I **(20)** _____ (not / do) it!'

 Use the past perfect to emphasize that one action occurred before another, e.g. *It was then that Holmes noticed the gun. It **had slipped** down the back of the sofa.*

9 Narrative tenses 2

Complete the story using the forms of the verbs to help you.

Post Office clerks, however busy, must always keep their wits about them. One of them **(1)** _____*h*_____ of the extraordinary mistakes that people sometimes make.

One day, the office **(2)** _____ was very busy and there were long queues at all the counters. People **(3)** _____ forms, writing cards and wrapping up parcels, and the counter staff were kept hard at work.

An old man, who **(4)** _____ to her, came in with a letter which he **(5)** _____ to his son in America. The clerk **(6)** _____ the cost of the postage and supplied the necessary stamps. The old man **(7)** _____ his glasses and to save time the clerk **(8)** _____ the stamps on the envelope for him. It was a good thing **(9)** _____ , for she discovered that the man **(10)** _____ letter to himself!

a	found out
b	had addressed
c	had forgotten
d	happened to be known
e	offered to stick
f	that she did
g	wanted to send
h	was telling me
i	were filling out
j	where she works

10 Future tenses 1

Put each sentence into the most suitable category. There is more than one example for some categories.

1	prediction	_e,_
2	schedule	_____
3	personal plan	_____
4	intention	_____
5	future fact	_____

a 'Are you ready? I will count to three …'

b 'Hurry up! The match starts at three o'clock and it's half past two already!'

c 'I'm going to finish this homework if it kills me!'

d 'I'm gonna sit right down and write myself a letter' (popular song)

e 'It's going to rain. Look at those clouds!'

f Most of my friends are running in the London marathon next Sunday.

g I'll be working in Dubai next summer.

h The President begins her tour of the Middle East next week.

i 'We're having a car-boot sale on Saturday. Why don't you come along?'

j 'Will you be able to give the children a lift?'

k 'You're never going to pass your exams if you spend all your time playing games on your computer!'

 Gonna is slang for *going to*.

11 Future tenses 2

Complete the dialogue using sentences (a–e) and an appropriate future form of the verb.

Joe: Hi Adrian! What are you doing?

1 **Adrian:** _____

Joe: When is it?

2 **Adrian:** _____

Why don't you come?

3 **Joe:** _____

Adrian: Give yourself a break, Joe!

4 **Joe:** _____

Adrian: I'll get you a free ticket.

5 **Joe:** _____

a I can't! _I'll be revising_ for my exams.

  a) I revise   b) I'm revising   c) I'll be revising

b It's on Saturday. _____ at eight o'clock and
  _____ until midnight.

  a) It starts ... and goes on   b) It will start ... and will go on

  c) It's starting ... and is going on

c I'm practising for the gig. _____ our best gig yet!

  a) It's going to be   b) It's   c) It will be

d Thanks, Adrian. _____ me a few quid!

  a) That's saving   b) That'll save   c) That saves

e I guess you're right. OK, _____ to the concert.

  a) I come   b) I'm coming   c) I'll come

- The future is uncertain, so our attitude to future events is important in helping us to decide which form to use: *will do*, *does*, *going to do*, etc. Sometimes we can use more than one future tense in a situation depending on what our attitude to the situation is. *Will* is often used to express simple statements of fact which are not coloured by our attitude, e.g. *The march **will** go ahead as planned.*

- *Quid* is a colloquial word for one pound sterling. *Gig* is an informal word for a jazz or pop music concert.

Section 2: Auxiliary verbs

Auxiliary verbs are 'helper' verbs. They are used mainly to form tenses, questions and negatives. The main auxiliary verbs are *be*, *do* and *have*, e.g. *I am going out now. Do you speak many languages? Had you been there before?* (There are also modal auxiliary verbs, see section 5.)

Do is also used to emphasize or contradict.
*I **do** wish you wouldn't whistle all the time!*
*Why didn't you send her a birthday card? But I **did** send her a card!*

QUESTION TAGS

Can Sam speak Italian? is a simple question, asking for information. We add a question tag to a statement in order to ask for confirmation or agreement. An affirmative sentence has a negative question tag, and a negative sentence has an affirmative question tag, e.g. *Sam **can** speak Italian, **can't** he? Sam **can't** speak Italian, **can** he?*

The verb in the tag is a reflection of the auxiliary or modal verb in the sentence, e.g. *He **will** help us, **won't** he? You **haven't** lost your glasses again, **have** you?* If there is no auxiliary or modal in the sentence, use part of *do* in the tag, e.g. *He **lives** in Spain, **doesn't** he? You **went** to Keele University, **didn't** you?*

'Sam can speak Italian, can't he?'

12 Questions and negatives

A Make questions using the words in brackets.

1 I like potatoes.

_____*Do you like potatoes*_____ ? (you)

2 He got a letter this morning.

_____ ? (you)

3 He studies physics.

_____ ? (you)

4 I heard a strange noise.

_____ ? (you)

5 My students are very clever.

_____ ? (your students)

6 Mary has read all the Harry Potter stories.

_____ ? (the other children)

7 Someone rang the doorbell.

_____ ? (you)

8 I need a glass of water.

_____ ? (anyone else)

B Complete the sentences using the verb in its negative form.

1 I like potatoes, but _____*I don't like*_____ cabbage.

2 I did the first test, but _____ the second one.

3 Dad has washed the car, but _____ the caravan.

4 He shook his head, but _____ my hand!

5 I've got two brothers, but _____ any sisters.

6 My parents speak Spanish, but _____ Catalan.

7 He was looking at me, but _____ listening to me.

8 My sister plays the piano, but _____ it very well!

13 Combinations

A   Choose a, b or c to complete the verb phrases.

(a) work   (b) working   (c) worked

1	I am not	_____b_____
2	I am	_____
3	I didn't	_____
4	I don't	_____
5	I have been	_____
6	I have	_____
7	I was	_____
8	I will	_____
9	will be	_____

B   Now use some of the above to complete the sentences.

1   I __*don't work*__ because I retired a year ago.

2   I had a good job, but it was an easy one so I _____ very hard!

3   My hobby is embroidery, and I _____ on a new pattern at the moment.

4   The weather's fine today so if you need me, I _____ in the garden.

5   I _____ on a plan for a new flower bed, but the ground was not suitable.

6   I _____ in the garden every day, but only when the weather is fine.

14 Question tags 1

Match each question tag with a phrase.

1	We need to pass the test,	a	haven't we?
2	We mustn't say that,	b	do we?
3	We've got to pay it all back,	c	must we?
4	We'll have to sell everything,	d	don't we?
5	We don't have to answer every question,	e	won't we?

6	They didn't need to be so rude,	f	aren't they?
7	They had to leave early,	g	didn't they?
8	They've had to make a lot of changes,	h	did they?
9	They're having to sell the business,	i	haven't they?
10	They'll have to get rid of the stock,	j	won't they?

11	Let's go,	k	can't you?
12	Put this in the fridge for me,	l	didn't he?
13	He used to be your secretary,	m	shall we?
14	They shouldn't be doing that,	n	will you?
15	Be quiet,	o	should they?

15 Question tags 2

Complete the captions using question tags and match them to the illustrations.

1

☐

2

☐

3

☐

4

☐

5

6

| | | |

a   You have been to France, _____*haven't you*_____ ?

b   You know my brother, _____ ?

c   So you passed your driving test, _____ ?

d   Your brother is getting married soon, _____ ?

e   You really don't understand what I am saying,
_____ ?

f   So the computer's crashed again, _____ ?

 When the speaker expresses surprise or anger, the form of the question tag can change to positive statement + positive tag e.g. *So you **think** you're better than me, **do** you?*

16 Joke time 1

Put the verbs in brackets into a suitable form to complete the jokes. In some cases, more than one tense will fit.

1 **Man:** What ____*do*____ you ___*get*___ if you cross an elephant and a mouse? (get)

Woman: Very big footprints in the margarine.

2 **Woman:** _____ you _____ the joke about the dustcart? (hear)

Man: Don't worry, it's a load of rubbish!

3 **Patient:** Doctor, Doctor I _____ my memory! (lose)

Doctor: When _____ this _____ ? (happen)

Patient: When did what happen?

4 **Man:** What _____ you _____ that little medal for? (get)

Woman: For singing.

Man: What _____ you _____ the big one for? (get)

Woman: For stopping!

5 **Mother:** Doctor, Doctor my son _____ my pen, what should I do? (swallow)

Doctor: Use a pencil till I get there.

6 **Man:** Why _____ elephants never _____ ? (forget)

Woman: Because nobody ever tells them anything.

7 **Woman:** My dog has no nose.

Man: How _____ he _____ ? (smell)

Woman: Terrible!

---

8 **Man:** What _____ you _____ a gorilla wearing ear-muffs? (call)

Woman: Anything you like, he can't hear you!

---

9 **Passerby:** Good morning. What _____ you _____ to catch? (try)

Fisherman: Idiots.

Passerby: _____ you _____ much luck so far? (have)

Fisherman: Yes, you're the third one this morning!

17 Crazy captions 1

Match the captions with the cartoons.

a   'Do be careful!'

b   'Let's leave now, shall we?'

c   'But I did chase the cat out of the garden!'

d   'So you'd like to be taller, would you?'

e   'Don't let on that I did it, will you?'

f   'It never used to be this quiet on a Saturday afternoon, did it?'

Section 3:
Tenses 2

CONDITIONALS

Sequences of tense are important in conditional sentences. Conditionals describe:

- the consequences of a real and possible action
  If you press this, you'll hear the music. You won't learn unless you study.
- the consequences of an action which is not real or probable
  If I had more time, I would visit you (but I **don't** have enough time, so I **won't**).
- the consequences of an action which did not in fact happen
  If I had had more time, I would have visited you (but I **didn't** have enough time, so I **didn't**).

Certain situations may require a different sequence:
If you had taken the job, you would use a computer every day (but you **didn't** take it, so you **won't** use a computer).
If you hadn't warned him, he wouldn't be alive today (but you **warned** him and he **is** alive today).

REPORTED SPEECH

The tense of a reporting verb influences the tense of the verb in the statement or question you are reporting.
(present) *He **has told** everyone that he **is** changing his job.*
(past)   *He **told** everyone he **was** changing his job.*
(present) *He **wants** to know where everyone **has gone**.*
(past)   *He **wanted** to know where everyone **had gone**.*

We may use the original tense of the statement we are reporting if we are talking about things which are still true, e.g. *The teacher **told** us that Mr Jones is leaving* (and it is true, he is leaving). We can put it into the past if we are not sure whether what we are reporting is true, e.g. *The teacher told us that Mr Jones was leaving* (it may or may not be true).

If you hadn't warned him, he wouldn't be alive today.

18 Conditionals

Choose the correct option to complete these sentences. In some cases more than one form may fit.

1 If you promise not to tell anyone, I ____*will take*____ you to the casino.

     (a) will take   b) take   c) am taking

2 If we _____ bad times, we wouldn't appreciate the good times.

     a) wouldn't have   b) didn't have   c) don't have

3 Did you hear about that terrible train crash? I'm lucky I cancelled my trip. If I _____ , I might have been on that train.

     a) hadn't   b) didn't   c) wouldn't

4 I wouldn't have crashed the car if that tree _____ there.

     a) would not be   b) was not   c) hadn't been

5 If you _____ your room to look nice, you should clean it yourself.

     a) would want   (b) want   c) will want

6 You won't become a good guitarist unless you _____ every day.

     a) practised   b) practise   c) will practise

7 What difference would it make if we _____ here or not?

     a) stayed   b) are staying   c) stay

8 If I _____ my life to live over again, I would do things very differently!

     a) would have   b) have had   c) had

Modals and imperatives occur in conditional sentences:

*If you wanted to be an astronaut, you **should** have studied physics.*

*If you need any information, you **can** ask that man over there.*

***Jump** up and down if you want to get warm!*

19 Conditionals in action

Complete the sentences using the illustrations to help you.

I mixed red and blue and got purple.

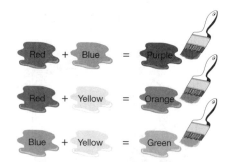

1 If you mix blue and yellow, <u>you get green</u> .

2 If you wanted orange, _____ !

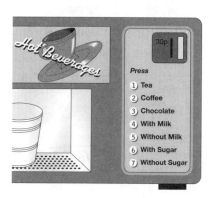

For tea without milk or sugar, press 1, 5 and 7.

3 If you want black coffee with sugar, _____ .

4 You can only get coffee with milk and sugar if _____ .

5 If you wanted chocolate without milk or sugar, you _____ 3, 5 and 7!

Multiply 12 by 3. The answer is 36.

6 You get the answer 4 if you _____ .

7 What do you get if you _____ ? 9.

$$12 \times 3 = 36$$
$$12 \div 3 = 4$$
$$12 + 3 = 15$$
$$12 - 3 = 9$$

The present tense is used in both parts of the conditional sentence to express something which is a fact or always true. In statements of cause and effect, both parts are in the present form, e.g. *If you **boil** water, it **turns** to steam.* This is because in these examples *if* means 'every time' or 'whenever'.

20 Reporting direct questions

Complete the sentences by reporting what was said.

1

'Where did that train come from?'

2

'What time did your son arrive home last night?'

3

'What time does the main feature begin?

4

'Shouldn't you take an umbrella in case it rains?'

5

'Have you found a pair that you like?'

1  Mother wants to know
where that train came from .

2  I asked the father

_____ .

3  I asked them what time

_____ .

4  He wondered whether we

_____ .

5  I simply asked her if

_____ .

- Avoid the common mistake of leaving the question in the direct form:
  ~~She asked me why didn't I speak~~. The correct form is *She asked me why
  I didn't speak*.
- Don't forget to make necessary changes to time expressions when
  reporting speech, e.g. *I finished it **yesterday***, but *He told us he had
  finished it **the day before***.

21 Reporting verbs

Complete the sentences reporting what was said. Use the forms of the verbs in the box to help you.

He admitted	He has promised
~~He warned him~~	She denied
She insisted that	She advised us

He warned him
it could cost a lot.

not to worry.

everything had to be ready
by six o'clock.

he didn't know where it was.

5

6

to love her forever.

doing it.

Verbs following reporting verbs fall into several different groups. The most common ones are:

1 Reporting verbs followed by *that* e.g. *agree, insist, persuade*. We **agreed that** *it wouldn't work!*

2 Reporting verbs which can be followed by *that* and a person e.g. *expect, promise, tell*. We **told you that** *it wouldn't work.*

3 Reporting verbs that are followed by a person and *to*, e.g. *advise, persuade, tell*. He **advised us to** *leave as soon as we could.*

4 Reporting verbs that can be followed by *should*, e.g. *advise, demand, suggest*. They **demanded that she should** *show her pass.*

22 What's the difference? 2

Match the headlines with the definitions.

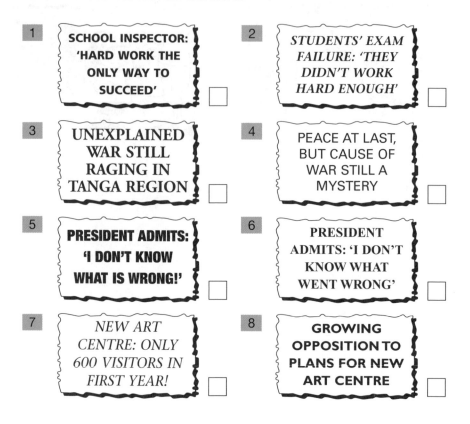

1 SCHOOL INSPECTOR: 'HARD WORK THE ONLY WAY TO SUCCEED'

2 *STUDENTS' EXAM FAILURE: 'THEY DIDN'T WORK HARD ENOUGH'*

3 UNEXPLAINED WAR STILL RAGING IN TANGA REGION

4 PEACE AT LAST, BUT CAUSE OF WAR STILL A MYSTERY

5 PRESIDENT ADMITS: 'I DON'T KNOW WHAT IS WRONG!'

6 PRESIDENT ADMITS: 'I DON'T KNOW WHAT WENT WRONG'

7 *NEW ART CENTRE: ONLY 600 VISITORS IN FIRST YEAR!*

8 GROWING OPPOSITION TO PLANS FOR NEW ART CENTRE

a The headline suggests that the students didn't work hard enough.

b The headline suggests that students should work harder!

c Nobody knew what the war had been about.

d Nobody knew what the war was about.

e The president said he wished he knew all the facts.

f The president said he wished he had known all the facts.

g The newspaper warned that the council should not waste money building a new Art Centre.

h The newspaper implied that the council should not have wasted money building a new Art Centre.

Section 4: Passives

The passive is made with a form of *be* + the past participle of the verb.
Everyone is invited (present simple passive).
Not a word was spoken (past simple passive).
Nothing has been decided (present perfect passive).
New houses are being built on the old airfield (present continuous passive).

Changing from active to passive is a way of showing what is most important in your mind:
Sir Alexander Fleming discovered penicillin in 1928.
(Active sentence, focus on Sir Alexander Fleming.)
Penicillin was discovered by Fleming in 1928.
(Passive sentence, focus on penicillin.)

If the agent is not known or not important, leave it out:
Penicillin was discovered in 1928.
The Rocky Mountains were formed over several millennia.

When a verb has two objects, as in *They gave each child a small gift*, either object can become the subject of the passive depending on which is more important to you:
A small gift was given to each child.
Every child was given a small gift.

'Everyone is invited!'

23 Passive forms

Rewrite these sentences in the passive.

1   The airline has announced a delay.

A delay ___*has been announced*___ .

2   Somebody wants you on the phone.

You _____ .

3   You must keep the documents in a safe place.

The documents _____ .

4   Is someone giving you a lift tonight?

Are you _____ .

5   They are going to replace the old town bridge soon.

The old town bridge _____ .

6   Has anybody delivered the mail yet?

Has the mail _____ ?

7   The receptionist told us to go to the waiting room.

We _____ .

8   If the garage had serviced the car properly, it wouldn't have broken down.

If the car _____ , it wouldn't have broken down.

9   You have to defrost the pizza before you cook it.

The pizza _____ .

24 What does it mean?

Say what these notices mean. The first one has been done as an example.

1

NO CHANGE GIVEN

2

RARE BOOKS BOUGHT

3

PETS **NOT** ALLOWED IN THIS RESTAURANT

4

ALL SALE ARTICLES REDUCED BY 40%

5

NO ADULTS ADMITTED IN THIS TOY SHOP
UNLESS **ACCOMPANIED BY A CHILD!**

1 This machine _____*doesn't give change*_____ .

2 We _____ .

3 You _____ .

4 The shop _____ .

5 We _____ .

The tense in the passive sentence is the same as in the active sentence:
*Thieves **have stolen** our garden gnomes* (present perfect).
*Our garden gnomes **have been stolen** by thieves* (present perfect passive).

25 Active or passive?

Complete the answers to the questions using the forms of the verbs to help you.

1 was asked / asked

   a What did the police say to you?

        ___*They asked me*___ to make a statement.

   b What happened to you at the police station?

        ___*I was asked*___ to make a statement.

2 have been promised / has promised

   a Are you getting more money next year?

        _____ a pay rise.

   b What has the boss said about our pay?

        _____ a pay rise.

3 going to be given / going to give

   a What is the teacher going to do next?

        _____ our new timetables.

   b What happens next?

        _____ our new timetables.

4 will be sent / will send

   a How will I hear about my exam results?

        _____ a letter.

   b Will the school let me know my results?

        _____ a letter.

5   were shown / showed

    a   What did you learn in cookery class today?

          _____ how to make an omelette.

    b   What did the cookery teacher do today?

          _____ how to make an omelette.

6   were told / told

    a   What did the receptionist say to you?

          _____ to wait outside.

    b   Why aren't you inside?

          _____ to wait outside.

'_____ *to wait outside.'*

You don't need to mention the person if you don't think it is important: *Everyone has been told (by the boss) not to leave our computers on overnight.* It might be obvious that only the boss gives orders!

26 What needs doing?

Say what the problem is in each picture. Use the pattern *need doing* and a verb from the box to help you.

> ~~cut~~   feed   iron   mend   rewrite   shorten   strengthen   sort

1

The grass needs cutting .

2

_____ .

3

_____ .

4

_____ .

5

_____ .

6

_____ .

7

_____ .

8

_____ .

 You can also use the passive infinitive after _need_, e.g. _The car **needs to be serviced**._

27 Have something done

Complete these dialogues with a verb and noun from the box, using the pattern *have something done* and making any necessary changes.

---

check   clean   ~~cut~~   examine   install   remove   service   steal
air-conditioning   car   carpet   ~~hair~~   old shed   teeth   wallet   wound

---

1   'John looks so untidy and scruffy!'
'Yes, he needs to _have his hair cut_ .'

2   'Your children have beautiful teeth! How come?'
'It's because they _____ every six months.'

3   'What are you going to do about your garden?'
'Well, for a start, I'm _____ .'

4   'What is wrong with her? She won't even let me in the house?'
'That's because she's _____ .'

5   'How was your holiday?'
'It was ruined because I _____ when I was in Barcelona.'

6   'How's the car running?'
'Great, I _____ a couple of days ago.'

7   'What happened?'
'I cut myself with a knife.'
'Well, you really ought _____ it looks infected.'

8   'You'll never stand the summer here in Nairobi!'
'Oh yes, we will. We're _____ before the hot season starts.'

Use the construction *have some thing done* when you don't intend to do it yourself but you intend to pay someone else to do it! You can also use the construction *get something done* with *must*, e.g. *I must get this suit dry-cleaned*.

Section 5: Modal verbs

The modal verbs tested in this section enable us to talk about:

Possibility
*You **might** just catch the bus if you hurry.*
*You **could** eat that snail, but I wouldn't recommend it!*
*Marco said he **may** call round later on.*

Ability
*I know a man who **can** speak the language of the ancient Egyptians, but he's sad because he's got nobody to talk to!*

Obligation or lack of obligation
*All candidates **must** bring their ID cards to the exam room.*
*The last bus had left so we **had to** walk home.*
*You **don't need to** write your name at the top of every page.*
*You **don't have to** wear a coat if you don't want to.*

Certainty
*You **must** be tired after doing nothing all day long.*
*That **can't** be John's handwriting; it's much too neat.*

Permission
***May** I borrow the car this evening, Mum?*
***Can** I park here?*

Advice and criticism
*You **should** cut down on smoking.*
*You **shouldn't** talk so loud.*

'You could eat that snail, but I wouldn't recommend it!'

28 *Should or should'nt?*

A Can you find the mistake in the following notices? Use *should* or *shouldn't* in your answers.

1

> **se habla inglés**
>
> **on parle anglais**
>
> **english spoken**

The word ___*English should*___ be written with a capital letter.

2

> **FRESH EGG'S**
> **FOR SALE**
> **AT BARGAIN**
> **PRICES**

The word _____ have an apostrophe.

3

> **CAR RENTALS**
> **£18 A DAY**
> **UNLIMITED MILLEAGE**

The word _____ be spelled with one 'l'.

B What are the people doing wrong? Use *should* or *shouldn't* in your answers.

1

He _____ .

2

The driver _____ the speed limit.

3

They _____ to each other.

Ought to is very similar in meaning to *should*. There is a very small difference in meaning: *should* suggests something we personally feel strongly about, e.g. *I really **should** call my parents*. The word *ought* suggests a duty we owe to others, not just to ourselves, e.g. *I **ought to** pay that bill.*

29 Can, could or be able to?

Complete these sentences using the forms of the verbs in the box to help you.

can	could	be able to	been able to	being able to

1 I used to __*be able to*__ speak Italian quite fluently when I was younger.

2 I _____ not see you tonight.

3 Have you _____ get any more information?

4 I'm sorry I _____ not come online earlier.

5 If you're short of money, I might _____ lend you some.

6 I _____ not find the bottle opener, so I just broke the top off.

7 I should _____ finish it by Friday.

8 It was terrible to be in the same room without _____ talk to you.

9 How did the thief get in without disturbing us? He must have _____ open the window without breaking the glass.

10 You _____ borrow my dictionary if you've lost yours.

11 Interpreters have to _____ translate without thinking

12 Do you think you will _____ finish on time?

The modal *can* has only one other form: the past form *could*. Otherwise use part of *be able to*, e.g. *I want* **to be able to** ... *I might* **be able to** ... There is no important difference of meaning between pairs like *I* **can** *do it* and *I am able to do it*; *I* **could** *meet you* and *I* **would be able to** *meet you*; **we couldn't go** and **we weren't able to go**.

30 Modal verbs of deduction

Complete the dialogue using the forms of the modal verbs in the box to help you.

must	must have	may	may have	can	can't	can't have	
	could	could have	might	might have			

Ann: What's that in the garden?

Joe: It **(1)** ___must be___ (be) a bird of some kind.

Ann: It **(2)** _____ (be) a bird. It's hasn't got any wings. Birds have wings.

Joe: It **(3)** _____ (be) a flightless bird like the ones they have in New Zealand.

Ann: It **(4)** _____ (be) from New Zealand, surely! I mean how did it get here?

Joe: It **(5)** _____ (fly) here, I suppose.

Ann: It **(6)** _____ (fly) here. It's flightless, remember!

Joe: You're right. It **(7)** _____ (escape) from a zoo. And then walked into our garden.

Ann: Do you think we ought to tell someone?

Joe: No, if we leave it alone, it **(8)** _____ just (fly away).

Ann: Don't you mean 'walk away'?

31 *Have to*

A Choose *a*, *b*, *c* or *d* to complete the verb phrases.

(a) have to   (b) to have to   (c) having to   (d) had to

1	will	___*a*___	**4**	has	_____
2	would have	_____	**5**	without	_____
3	used	_____	**6**	might	_____

B Now use the verb forms above to complete the sentences.

1 Harry's boss is away: it's the first time he __*has had to*__ run the office himself.

2 When we were children, we _____ get up at five o'clock every morning.

3 I _____ spend the night at Janet's house; it depends when the party finishes!

4 I _____ walk home if you hadn't been there.

5 Jane isn't here: she _____ go to Head Office for another meeting.

6 Even if you're in a hurry, you _____ wait your turn like everyone else!

7 I wish the children would put their things away without _____ be reminded all the time.

8 I hope it won't be necessary, but I _____ ask you to lend me some money.

The modal *must/mustn't* has no other form, i.e. it is used for the present simple only. All other forms are made up of parts of *have to*, e.g. *we **had to** go by bus*; *I will **have to** leave soon*.

32 *Must* or *have to*?

Complete these sentences using a form of *have to* or *must*. In some cases, more than one form may fit.

1   Helen's very busy: she **_has had to_** attend five conferences this month.

2   I see you've had another accident. You really _____ be more careful in future!

3   How many people took part in the London Marathon? It _____ be over 25,000!

4   Michael might _____ go to the hospital next week for a check-up.

5   How are you today, Mrs Smith? Not too bad, thank you. I _____ complain!

6   I know you have to practise to become a professional drummer, but you _____ make so much noise, surely?

7   You _____ be surprised if the boss suddenly throws a book at you. It's just his way of keeping the employees on their toes!

8   There is a sign in the office which says 'You _____ be mad to work here, but it helps!'

9   There was only a short queue so we _____ wait long.

10   Tenants _____ keep pets in the house.

- There is a slight difference of meaning between *I must go* and *I have to go*. The form *must* suggests an obligation you place on yourself, e.g. *I really must learn to make better use of my time!* The form *have to* suggests an obligation placed on you by others, e.g. *I'd love to stay and talk to you, but I have to go to see my boss at 2 o'clock.*
- *Mustn't* means you are obliged not to do something, e.g. *you mustn't talk in the library.*
  Don't have to means you are not obliged, e.g. *you don't have to talk if you don't want to.*
- *Needn't* or *don't need to* both mean that you are not obliged, or it is not necessary for you to do something, e.g. *You needn't wait for us, we'll catch up with you later.*

33 Crazy captions 2

Match the captions with the cartoons.

1

2

3

4

5

6

a   It must have been a very high tide!

b   You don't have to shout, sir. I'm not deaf, you know!

c   You shouldn't have used so much soap powder!

d   You'll be able to get on if you run fast and then jump!

e   Why can't you breed chickens like other poultry farmers?

f   I know, I know, you don't need to keep reminding me!

Section 6: Verb phrases

The most common patterns are:

Verb + preposition

A number of verbs can be followed by a preposition, e.g. *believe* (*in*), *depend* (*on*), *worry* (*about*). In some cases, a verb can take more than one preposition with a change of meaning, e.g. *Do you agree **with** me? The union has agreed **to** the new overtime schedule.*

Phrasal verbs

These are two- or three-word verbs.

| verb + adverb | e.g. *fall out* (quarrel) |
| verb + preposition | e.g. *take after* (resemble) |

The meaning is not always easy to derive from the individual words in the verb, e.g. *take someone off* means to 'impersonate'.

If the phrasal verb is a verb + adverb, the object may come before or after the adverb, e.g. ***look up the word*** *in a dictionary* or ***look the word up*** *in a dictionary*. If the object is a pronoun it must come before the adverb, e.g. ***look it up*** *in the dictionary*, not ~~*look up it*~~. If the phrasal verb is a verb + preposition, the object always comes after the preposition, e.g. *she takes after **her father*** or *she takes after **him***. Check the use of each individual verb in a good dictionary.

She takes after her father.

34 Phrasal verbs 1

Replace the words in bold type with a phrasal verb to complete the grid.

1. I **happened to find** this old painting while I was browsing in an antiques shop the other day.

2. Should we stop now or **continue**?

3. They said rollerblading would never **become popular** in this country!

4. We were late for the meeting because we were **delayed** in the traffic.

5. Here's a crossword clue. Can you **solve** it?

6. I usually work until six o'clock, but I'm going to try to **leave** early today.

7. If you're not in a hurry, why don't you **come and see us** on your way home?

8. We didn't finish our telephone conversation because we were suddenly **disconnected**.

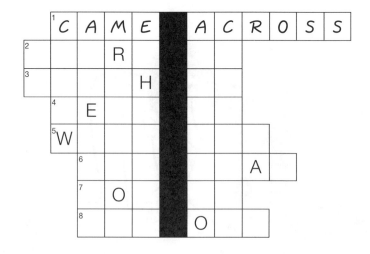

35 Phrasal verbs 2

A Complete the grid to make as many correct phrasal verbs as you can.

	away	down	in	off	up
break					
come					
give	✓	✗	✓	✓	✓
keep					
fall					
shut					

B Replace the words in bold type with a verb from the table above. Write the verb in the appropriate form.

1 Marca and Fred had a fight, but he wouldn't **surrender** even when she sat on his head!   _give in_

2 The club was losing money, so in the end the owners **closed** it.   _____

3 Whenever the subject of nuclear power **arises**, people seem to get very angry.   _____

4 People were advised to **avoid visiting** the city centre during the rush hour.   _____

5 Attendance at our local football matches has been **declining** lately.   _____

6 Without warning, he **lost his self-control** and burst into tears.   _____

> Remember that sometimes the particle can have a meaning:
> *down* = from a high point to a lower one, e.g. cut **down** a tree
> *off* = down or away from, e.g. take something **off** a shelf
> *up* = completely, e.g. eat **up** all your vegetables.

36 Three-word verbs

Replace the words in bold type with a verb from the box, making any necessary changes.

boil down to	~~do away with~~	fall back on	fall behind with
go back on	get away with	look back on	run out of

1 Most states in the US have **abolished** the death penalty.

done away with

2 If you **fail to meet** the payments on the car, the company will come and repossess it.

_____

3 If the computer crashes, there's always paper and pencil to **use as a temporary solution**.

_____

4 An old man swallowed a potion to make himself invisible and then walked into a bank to steal some money. It was a good plan, but he didn't **succeed** because his briefcase was still visible!

_____

5 The minister is an honest man. He would never **break** his word, would he?

_____

6 I saw a sign outside a restaurant which said: 'We will make any meal you want. If we can't, we'll give you ten pounds!'

I asked for elephant's eyeballs on toast. The manager gave me ten pounds, saying:

'Sorry, sir, we **have no** bread **left**!'

_____

7 I am sure we will all **recall** this special occasion with fond memories.

_____

8 The situation seems complicated, but what it **really means** is that we haven't got any money left!

_____

37 Verbs with following preposition 1

A   Complete the grid by matching each verb with its preposition.

	about	**from**	**in**	**on**
believe	✗	✗	✓	✗
congratulate				
depend				
differ				
enquire				
joke				
prevent				
rely				
suffer				
worry				

B   Complete the sentences using some of the above verbs and making any necessary changes.

1   'Do you think that there are such things as ghosts?'

He asked me ___*if I believed in ghosts*___ .

2   'You've won first prize, Linda! Well done!'

The judge _____ .

3   'Can you tell me the times of morning trains to Portsmouth?'

He was _____ .

4   Ali is a very dependable sort of guy.

You can _____ .

5   He takes painkillers because he has terrible headaches.

He takes painkillers because he _____ .

38 Verbs with following preposition 2

Match each verb with its preposition. Choose from the four possible answers.

1 John apologised ___*for*___ being late.

   a) for   b) of   c) to   d) with

2 I intend to apply _____ a job in the Accounts Department.

   a) from   b) in   c) for   d) with

3 Sarah is finding it difficult to cope _____ her three small babies.

   a) for   b) of   c) with   d) about

4 I object _____ people smoking in restaurants.

   a) from   b) about   c) of   d) to

5 Groucho Marx said he wouldn't want to belong _____ a club which would have him as a member!

   a) in   b) to   c) with   d) for

6 Water consists _____ two hydrogen atoms and one oxygen atom.

   a) in   b) from   c) of   d) with

7 Ballroom dancing only appeals _____ older people, doesn't it?

   a) for   b) on   c) by   d) to

8 According to the bank statement, we spent 900 pounds this month, but I can only account _____ 895 pounds.

   a) for   b) from   c) to   d) with

Section 7: Verb patterns

The following patterns occur:

- Verbs which are followed by the -ing form of the verb, e.g. *He dislikes making small talk. I enjoy skiing. I keep getting these numbers confused.* This –ing form behaves like a noun: *I like jogging, I like sport, I like it.*

- Verbs which are followed by the to-infinitive, e.g. *I agreed to help him. Don't hesitate to ask for help. We're longing to see you again!* Note also the use of verb + to-infinitive to express intention, e.g. *A man from the council came to inspect the premises.*

- Verbs which can be followed by the -ing form or to-infinitive. Some have a great difference of meaning, e.g. *Stop talking!* and *We stopped to have a rest.* Some have only a slight difference of meaning, e.g. *I hate getting up early* or *I hate to get up early. It started to rain* or *it started raining.*

- Verbs which are followed by the -ing form of the verb or the infinitive without to, e.g. *I heard a door close* or *I heard someone singing.* For the difference, see the tip box to Test 41.

We stopped to have a rest.

39 Verb patterns 1

There is a mistake in the verb pattern in some of the following sentences. Correct the sentence if necessary. The first two have been done as examples.

1   Charlie is the sort of man who hates being criticized.

2   I started work when I was sixteen, and now I'm in a dead-end job. I really regret not to stay on at college to get a qualification.

3   We've worked all morning. Shall we stop having lunch now?

4   Do you work here? I don't remember seeing you before.

5   When you have finished to wash the dishes, you can clean the kitchen floor.

6   Would you mind making me a cup of coffee, please?

7   Don't bother to get up, I can see myself out.

8   As we are all very tired, I suggest to leave everything as it is and we'll do the rest tomorrow morning.

9   I need painting the outside of the house before winter comes.

10   If you like tongue twisters, try saying 'Six Swiss wristwatches'!

1	✓	6	_____
2	*regret not staying*	7	_____
3	_____	8	_____
4	_____	9	_____
5	_____	10	_____

Note the difference between *try to do* and *try doing*. *Try to do* means see if you can or cannot do something, e.g. *Try to lift this log!* (Let's see how strong you are!); *trying doing* means see if doing something will solve a problem, e.g. *If you can't open the lock with the key, try opening it with a paper clip.*

40 Verb patterns 2

Complete these sentences using the verb in capital letters followed by a verb which fits the meaning of the sentence. The first one has been done as an example.

1 If you have difficulty pronouncing the letter 'h',
___*practise saying*___ 'He hit her on her hairy
head with a hard, heavy hammer'!   PRACTISE

2 Don't _____ your mobile phone
in case you need to phone me.   FORGET

3 Police have asked motorists to _____
into the city centre by car during peak hours.   AVOID

4 Did you _____ a birthday card
for your sister?   REMEMBER

5 When I saw Janet's husband doing handstands in
the street, I couldn't _____ Janet
what I had seen.   RESIST

6 Sophie _____ the chocolate, even
though she had chocolate all round her mouth.   DENY

7 David _____ a stone out of his
shoe, and then carried on walking.   STOP

8 I don't _____ you permission to
use my computer!   REMEMBER

9 Take this coffee to your grandad. The cup is rather
full, so _____ not
_____ any on the carpet!   TRY

10 I'm going to get fit for the London Marathon, even if
it _____ twenty kilometres a day!   MEAN

41 Crazy captions 3

Complete the captions using a suitable form of the verb in brackets and match them with the cartoons.

1

2

3

4

5

6

a   I thought I could see something ___*moving*___ in the trees. (move)

b   Can you hear someone _____ ? (snore)

c   Did you hear a gun _____ ? (go off)

d   Don't let me catch you _____ my clothes again! (wear)

e   I wish you wouldn't keep _____ me. (interrupt)

f   Did anyone see him _____ the house? (leave)

There is an important difference between *I heard someone sing* and *I heard someone singing*. The infinitive suggests that you witnessed the whole action from start to finish; the -ing form suggests that you heard the action in progress.

42 Verb patterns crossword

Complete the clues to the crossword using the verbs in the box in a suitable form. Some of the answers may have two words.

Across

| fail | ~~get~~ | intend | lie | own | ring | sing | take | want |

1. I won't take the 'red eye flight' if it means _____ up early in the morning.

6. Look at that ugly building! It makes me _____ to scream!

7. 'Let sleeping dogs _____.' (proverb)

9   'The road to hell is paved with good intentions.'
    I don't _____ to take any notice of that proverb!

11 I'd rather _____ than spend my life never taking risks.

13 And now, ladies and gentlemen, I'd like _____ twelve
    Schuber *lieder* for you.

15 Would you rather _____ your house instead of just renting it?

17 You should avoid _____ sides in your friends' arguments.

18 Can you hear a bell _____ ? It's coming from the house next
    door.

Down

| file   go off   go   invent   lose   need   notice   stir   wait   walk |

1   We heard a gun _____ in the distance.

2   We were advised _____ for the snow to stop before setting
    out.

3   I couldn't help _____ that you are wearing odd socks.

4   Why don't you have someone _____ those letters instead of
    doing it yourself?

5   After all this rain, the lawns will soon _____ cutting again.

8   If you haven't got an excuse for not doing your essay, you'd
    better _____ one quickly!

10 Would you care _____ for a drive in my new car?

12 It's no use _____ your temper, it will just make things worse.

14 Did I just see you _____ your coffee with a pencil? Why
    don't you use a spoon like other people?

16 Let's _____ to the shops! The exercise will do us good!

Section 8: Word building

PREFIXES AND SUFFIXES

Many verbs can be formed from other words by using prefixes or suffixes.

Prefixes are put in front of the word to change the meaning of that word.
co- + *exist = coexist*
en- + *courage = encourage*
fore- + *tell = foretell*

Suffixes can be put at the end of the word to make a verb, for example:
false + -**ify** = *falsify*
private + -**ize** = *privatize*
hard + -**en** = *harden*

All these affixes have meaning, for example: the prefix **fore-** means before, as in ***fore**see* (predict); **mis-** means bad, wrong or not, as in ***mis**understand* (understand incorrectly); **un-** means not or the opposite, as in ***un**tie* (reversing the action of tying); **over-/under-** mean too much or not enough, as in ***over**cook* or ***under**cook* (cook too much or too little). Similarly, the suffixes -**ify**, -**ize** and -**en** mean make or become as in *fals**ify*** (make false); *dramat**ize*** (make dramatic, turn something into a play); *length**en*** (make long or longer).

CONSONANT CLUSTERS

There are also clusters of initial or final letters, such as **gl-** or **–kle**. These clusters hint at meaning: the **gl-** in *gleam*, *glow*, *glitter* is to do with quality of light; the -**kle** in *crackle*, *sparkle*, *twinkle* is to do with a repeated small action.

Over-/under- *mean too much or too little, as in* ***overcook*** *or* ***undercook***.

43 Verbs beginning with em- or en-

A   Match each verb with its definition.

1	enrich	a	apply a law or rule
2	enable	b	give support to
3	enclose	c	surround
4	encourage	d	put in an envelope or letter
5	endanger	e	give power or authority to
6	enforce	f	make bitter
7	enlarge	g	make bigger
8	empower	h	make certain
9	embitter	i	make possible
10	ensure	j	make richer or better
11	encircle	k	put at risk

B   Complete these sentences with some of the above verbs, making any necessary changes.

1   Did you know that plutonium is simply __*enriched*__ uranium?

2   From an early age, Mozart was _____ by his father to compose music.

3   Please find _____ a copy of my CV.

4   There is no point in passing laws that cannot be _____ .

5   The black rhino is an _____ species: there are only a few left in the wild.

6   I intend to get this photograph of our local football team _____ so that I can frame it and hang it over my bed.

7   Please _____ that your seatbelts are fastened and your seat is in the upright position.

8   The driving mirror in a car _____ you to see what is behind you without having to turn your head.

The prefix **en-** changes to **em-** before **b** and **p** for ease of pronunciation.

44 Word building

A   Complete the table with the appropriate forms of the words.

	ADJECTIVE	VERB	NOUN
1	apologetic	*apologize*	apology
2	broad		
3			criticism
4	economic(al)		
5	false		
6	fat		fat
7			generalization
8	legal		
9			maximum
10	moist		
11	public		publicity
12	pure		purity
13			sensation
14	specific		
15	standard		
16	sympathetic		sympathy
17	terrifying		
18	weak		weakness

B Now complete these sentences with verbs from the table, making any necessary changes.

1 He told me to meet him at the airport, but he didn't
___*specify*___ which terminal.

2 The only way to _____ is by spending less!

3 It's a good idea to praise students sometimes instead of always
_____ them!

4 We should try to _____ the use of the lecture theatre;
at the moment it is only used twice a week at the most.

5 The saying goes: 'Travel _____ the mind', but it is
only true if you have an open mind in the first place.

6 Big dogs with big teeth _____ me, but little dogs
don't scare me at all.

7 The farmers give the turkeys lots of corn to _____
them up for Christmas.

45 Verbs from adjectives and nouns

A Make verbs from the words.

1	blood	_____	5	long	_____
2	breath	_____	6	simple	_____
3	deep	_____	7	strong	_____
4	food	*feed*	8	wide	_____

B Now use the above verbs to complete the sentences.

'What do you
_____ *feed* _____ them on?'

'This skirt is too short,
I need to _____ it.'

'The water here is very
shallow; they'll need to
_____ the channel!'

'Put your finger on it,
then it won't _____ .'

5

'With all this heavy traffic,
you'd think they'd
_____ the bridge.'

6

'It's very complicated.
I wish they would
_____ it a bit!'

7

'Well, they did say they
needed to _____
the road.'

8

'If you _____
through your mouth, you
won't have any problems.'

 Note the changes of spelling that are sometimes needed, e.g. *long – length
– lengthen*; *simple – simplify*.

46 Verb families 1

A   Match each verb with its definition.

1	crumble	a	break into small pieces
2	fumble	b	come close to falling
3	grumble	c	fall in a heap
4	mumble	d	climb or crawl hurriedly
5	ramble	e	complain
6	scramble	f	shake from fear or cold
7	stumble	g	speak too softly to be heard
8	tremble	h	try unsuccessfully to hold or catch something
9	tumble	i	walk for pleasure

B   Now use some of the above verbs to complete the sentences, making any necessary changes.

1   He just ___*mumbled*___ under his breath so I couldn't understand a word he said.

2   John _____ but managed to keep his balance.

3   We found a photograph album in the attic, but it was so old that it just _____ as soon as we tried to turn the pages.

4   This is the wettest winter on record. Everyone is _____ about the weather.

5   When I picked up the injured bird, it was _____ with fear.

6   We watched the children as they _____ up the side of the hill.

47 Verb families 2

A   All these verbs describe qualities of light or ways of looking. Match each verb with its definition.

1	glance	a	shine faintly or intermittently
2	glare	b	get a brief passing view of
3	gleam	c	look briefly at
4	glimpse	d	give out a hard light; stare in an unfriendly way
5	glisten	e	shine with an intense heat
6	glitter	f	shine as a wet or oily surface does
7	glow	g	sparkle with light

B   Now use each of the above verbs to complete the sentences, making any necessary changes.

1   My glass smashed when I accidentally dropped it. My father ___*glared*___ at me, but didn't say anything.

2   The brass saucepan had been polished until it _____ .

3   'All that _____ is not gold.' (proverb)

4   I knew she was anxious to leave by the way she kept _____ at her watch.

5   'I know a tear would _____ , if once more I could listen to the gang that sang Heart of my Heart.' (popular song)

6   It was such a romantic scene, with the light from the moon _____ on the sea.

7   Don't put the meat on the barbecue until the coals are _____ .

48 Common verb prefixes 1

Replace the words in bold type using the verb in brackets and the appropriate prefix from the box. The first one has been done as an example.

co-   de-   dis-   over-   un-   under-

1 It's hot in here: why don't you **undo the buttons** on your shirt? (button)   *unbutton*

2 I'm sure the shop **made me pay too much.** (charge)   _____

3 **Take everything out of** your suitcase. (pack)   _____

4 All my pens have **vanished.** I can't find one anywhere! (appear)   _____

5 I'm sorry I'm late: I **did not wake up at my usual time.** (sleep)   _____

6 I've just taken this chicken and mushroom pie out of the oven, do I need to let it **thaw completely** before I cook it? (frost)   _____

7 If you **do not carry out** your orders, you will be punished. (obey)   _____

8 Let's try to learn to **work together** instead of fighting each other! (operate)   _____

9 SZKKB YRIGSWZB – can you **work out the
meaning of** this message? By the way, it's
my birthday today! (code)   _____

10 I may **not have the same opinion** as you,
but you have the right to say what you
think. (agree)   _____

11 Avoid meat that is **too rare**. (cook)   _____

12 The State of California decided to **remove
the regulations from** the electricity industry
with the result that prices went up over 300%
in one year. (regulate)   _____

13 A crazy driver **came level with and passed**
me on a blind bend today. He must think he
has X-ray eyes to see round corners! (take) _____

14 Tricia and Louise **wrote** a book **together**.
(author)   _____

15 The plane came in so fast that it **went
beyond the end of** the runway. (shoot)   _____

16 Is it possible for humans and animals to **share
the planet**? (exist)   _____

- co- means with or together, as in *co-operate*, *coexist*.
- re- means again or repeatedly, as in *reread*, *rewrite*, *reconsider*.

49 Prefix crossword

Complete the clues to the crossword using verbs which have a prefix.

Clues

Across

2 If you don't make the bed, it will stay _____ (6)

5 Don't throw that old envelope away, you can _____ it. (5)

6 If you pay too much for something, you _____ (7)

7 If you want to make people obey the law, you have to _____ it. (7)

9 The opposite of 'plug'. (6)

10 If you cast the wrong actor in a role, we say that the actor is _____ (7)

Down

1 If a competition football match ends in a draw, there has to be a _____ (6)

3 To pronounce a word wrongly is to _____ it. (12)

4 To go through an event, such as an accident, again in your mind. (6)

6 A feeling of sadness came over me: I was _____ by sadness. (8)

8 When the tenants moved out of the house, the letting agents _____ it (5).

Where the prefix **co-** is used with a word beginning with **o**, many people prefer to insert a hyphen to make the word clearer, e.g. *co-operate* instead of *cooperate*. Similarly with **re-** before an **e**, e.g. *re-enter* instead of *reenter*. In front of other vowels there is no clear rule, e.g. you can write *co-exist* or *coexist*, but it is best to avoid the hyphen except where confusion might occur, e.g. *re-cover* (put a new cover on) and *recover* (get better).

50 Common verb prefixes 2

A Combine the verbs with the prefixes. Some verbs may take more than one prefix.

	fore-	mis-	out-	re-
1 build	✗	✗	✗	*rebuild*
2 do				
3 grow				
4 lead				
5 pay				
6 read				
7 see				
8 take				
9 tell				
10 write				

B Now use some of the above verbs to complete the sentences. Use the verb in brackets to help you.

1 'Do you think Rachel deliberately _____ us when she said she was going to marry a prince? It turns out she's married a man called Michael Prince!' (lead)

2 This outfit doesn't fit my baby any more. I bought it only a month ago, and she's already _____ it. (grow)

3 My essay was full of spelling mistakes so the teacher made me _____ the whole thing. (write)

4 John owed his mother a thousand pounds, and he has _____ every penny. (pay)

5 Nostradamus predicted many things; he even _____ the two world wars of the twentieth century. (tell)

Section 9: Choosing the right verb

CONFUSING VERBS

There are many pairs or groups of verbs which can be confused.

Sometimes the confusion arises from verbs which are similar to ones in other languages, but have a different meaning in English (so-called 'false friends'), such as *control*. In English *control* means to 'be in charge of' or 'have power over', e.g. *The people who **control** the money **control** the world*. However, the French verb *contrôler*, the Italian *controllare*, and the German *kontrollieren* translate as check, e.g. *My job is to check all the company accounts to make sure there are no errors*.

Sometimes the confusion arises from verbs which basically have the same meaning, but are used in different contexts. For example, *begin* and *start* mean the same, but only one can be used in a particular context: you can ***start** to laugh* or ***begin** to laugh*, but you can only ***start** a machine*.

In some cases there are differences in the way the verbs behave grammatically, e.g. *say* and *tell*. You ***tell** me something*, but you ***say** something to me*.

SET EXPRESSIONS

There are many set expressions, combining verbs with other words:
- Verb + singular noun (often without *the*)
e.g. *catch sight of, start from scratch, take advantage, foot the bill*
- Verb + plural noun (often without *the*)
e.g. *change places, cut corners, go halves, make amends*
- Verb + adjective:
e.g. *go sour, come true, keep quiet*

foot the bill

51 *Make* or *do*?

Complete these dialogues with a suitable form of *make* or *do*.

1

Man: Did you **(a)** _make_ an appointment with the optician?

Woman: Oh, I forgot! Would you **(b)** _____ me a big favour? Could you **(c)** _____ a call to her receptionist and see if she can fit me in before the end of the week?

2

Man: Did you hear that Alpha Couriers **(a)** _____ a two million pound profit last year?

Woman: Wow! That's a firm I **(b)** _____ a lot of business with. Maybe I should try to buy the company!

Man: You mean, like The Godfather: 'You'll **(c)** _____ them an offer they can't refuse!'

3

Man: Did I tell you Linda and I had a row? I accused her of having an affair with someone else. I **(a)** _____ such a fuss! I **(b)** _____ a complete fool of myself! It wasn't even true.

Woman: Why don't you tell her you're sorry? It won't **(c)** _____ any harm, and it might even **(d)** _____ some good.

4

Man: I've got a terrible headache!

Woman: Try standing on your head for five minutes: that ought to **(a)** _____ the trick!

Man: That won't **(b)** _____ any difference. It'll just **(c)** _____ things worse.

Woman: Can I **(d)** _____ another suggestion?

Man: Please don't! I don't like '**(e)** _____ -it-yourself' remedies anyway.

52 *Say, speak, talk or tell?*

A Complete the sentences with a suitable form of *say, speak, talk* or *tell*.

a Yes, but he has nothing to ___say___ in any of them!

b I don't know, she didn't _____ me her name.

c Yes, he _____ his first word this morning.

d Well, I don't _____ lies if that's what you mean.

e What does she _____ about?

f Really? But who do you _____ to?

g You do _____ rubbish sometimes, dear!

h Don't worry, I wasn't _____ anything important!

i I'm sorry, could you _____ the name again? I didn't quite catch it.

j Not at all! He never stops _____ !

B Look at the sentences 1–10 and write the letter of the appropriate reply (a–j) in the speech bubble. The first one has been done as an example.

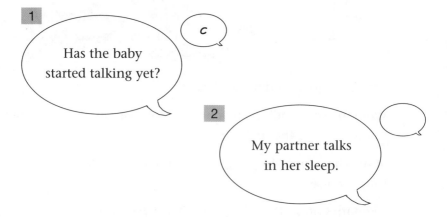

1

c

Has the baby started talking yet?

2

My partner talks in her sleep.

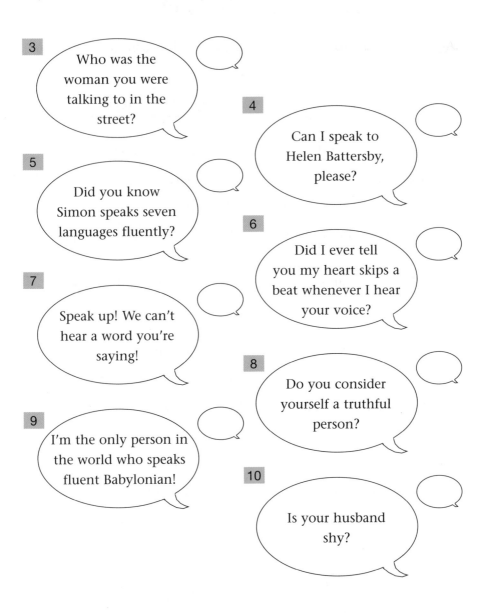

3 Who was the woman you were talking to in the street?

4 Can I speak to Helen Battersby, please?

5 Did you know Simon speaks seven languages fluently?

6 Did I ever tell you my heart skips a beat whenever I hear your voice?

7 Speak up! We can't hear a word you're saying!

8 Do you consider yourself a truthful person?

9 I'm the only person in the world who speaks fluent Babylonian!

10 Is your husband shy?

Speak and *talk* are not the same: speaking is a physical ability: you can **speak** a *foreign language*; talking is the use you make of that physical ability: you can **talk** *in a foreign language*. *Speak* is also used in the sense of *make a speech*.

53 Expressions with *take* or *have*

A Match each expression with its definition and write the answers in the grid below.

1	have second thoughts	**a**	be allowed to give your opinion
2	have a hard time	**b**	win an argument
3	have fun	**c**	change your mind, reconsider
4	have a bone to pick	**d**	enjoy yourself
5	have the last word	**e**	have something to argue about
6	have your say	**f**	experience difficulties
7	take a long look	**g**	examine
8	take care	**h**	not be in a hurry
9	take it easy	**i**	put yourself in danger
10	take something badly	**j**	react badly
11	take risks	**k**	relax
12	take your pick	**l**	pay attention
13	take your time	**m**	be cautious
14	take notice	**n**	have whatever you want

1	2	3	4	5	6	7	8	9	10	11	12	13	14
c													

B   Now use some of the above expressions to replace the words in bold
type in these sentences, making any necessary changes.

1   I had more or less made up my mind
about changing my job, but then
**I decided maybe it wasn't such a
good idea after all**.   *had second thoughts*

2   You've won! There's a variety of prizes:
you can **choose any one of them**.   _____

3   Drivers are requested to **be very
cautious** when driving through
a built-up area.   _____

4   After a really hard day at the office,
I like to **relax and put my feet up**.   _____

5   It was a very democratic meeting:
everyone was allowed to **express
their opinions**.   _____

6   Stuntmen in movies really do **put
their lives in danger** sometimes.   _____

7   I hear you are going to Ibiza for
your holidays. I'm sure you will
enjoy yourselves!   _____

8   Listen, Charlie, I **want to talk to**
you: why do you keep telling
everybody that I never take a bath?   _____

54 Confusing verbs

Choose between the verbs to complete the sentences, making any necessary changes.

1   hope/want/wish

    a   I ___wish___ I could come to the christening, but I won't be here.

    b   I ___hope___ I will be able to come to the christening.

2   bring/fetch/take

    a   Get out and _____ your things with you!

    b   Come to my place and _____ your things with you!

3   like/want/wish

    a   I _____ someone to buy me a dog for my birthday.

    b   I _____ someone would buy me a dog for my birthday.

4   recall/remember/remind

    a   ' _____ me to get a card for Mother's Day.'

       'Yes, Dad.'

    b   'Dad, did you _____ to get a Mother's Day card?'

       'It's a bit late to _____ me now! Mother's Day was last Sunday!'

5   intend/mean/think

    a   What makes you _____ that the environment will be an important issue in the next election?

    b   It depends what you _____ by that.

6   get/go/travel

    a   Does this bus _____ to Norwich?

    b   What time does the bus _____ to Norwich?

---

7   fail/pass/take

    a   'When is your final examination?'

       'I _____ it tomorrow.'

    b   'Have you had the results of your exam yet?'

       'Yes, unfortunately I _____ .'

'What time does the bus _____ to Norwich?'

Note how the words sometimes have different grammatical patterns as well as differences of meaning, e.g. *buy something*, but *pay for something*.

55 Confusing pairs

Look at the verbs in bold type and decide if the correct verb has been used.
Correct the sentence if necessary. The first two have been done as examples.

1   wear/carry

'Why do you always **carry** your coat over your arm?'

'Because it doesn't fit me!'

2   keep/hold

Why are you **keeping** a gun in your hand?

3   lie/lay

I **lay** on my bed and looked at the ceiling.

4   lose/waste

Don't **waste** time regretting what is past. Think of what you will
do tomorrow!

5   buy/pay

If you **pay** the drinks, I'll **pay** for the food.

6   rob/steal

The burglar was so disgusted with my cheap jewellery that he
decided not to **rob** it. Instead he left a ten-pound note and a
message that read: 'Buy yourself something decent!'

7   expect/wait for

Why don't you ask him for a dance? Go on! What are you
expecting?

8   hear/listen to

I could **hear** people talking in the next room, but I didn't bother to **hear** what they were saying.

9   feel/touch

Just **touch** how thick this piece of cloth is!

10   let/make

If I promise not to be a nuisance, will you **let** me stay up to watch the late movie?

11   cry/shout

There's no need to **cry**. I'm not deaf, you know!

12   begin/start

Tell me, how do you **begin** a car engine when you've lost the key?

1	✓	**7**	
2	*holding*	**8**	
3		**9**	
4		**10**	
5		**11**	
6		**12**	

Note the difference between *see* and *look/watch*. You *look* (or *watch*) because you make a conscious decision to observe something. You *see* simply because your eyes came to rest on something. The same difference occurs with *hear* and *listen*.

56 Crazy captions 4

A Match the verbs on the left with the plural nouns on the right.

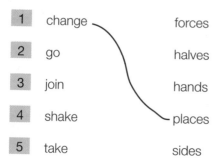

1	change	forces
2	go	halves
3	join	hands
4	shake	places
5	take	sides

B Now use the phrases to complete the captions for the cartoons making any necessary changes.

1 It might be better if we ____*change places*____ , dear.

2 Let's _____ , it's only fair!

3   Do you think we could beat them if we _____ ?

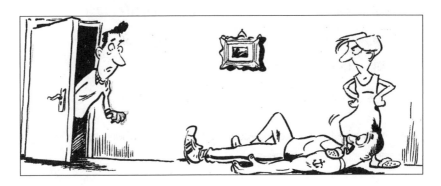

4   Well, I never like to _____ in a quarrel, but I do
    think in this case your wife is in the right.

5   I want to be friendly, but the thing is, how do you
    _____ with it?

57 Verb and noun

A Match the verbs on the left with the words on the right.

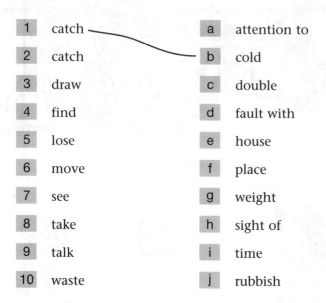

1	catch	a	attention to
2	catch	b	cold
3	draw	c	double
4	find	d	fault with
5	lose	e	house
6	move	f	place
7	see	g	weight
8	take	h	sight of
9	talk	i	time
10	waste	j	rubbish

B Now use the above expressions to complete these sentences, making any necessary changes.

1 It's bitterly cold out! Wrap up well, we don't want you to
_____*catch cold*_____ , do we?

2 If you go on a slimming diet, it must be obvious to everyone that
you are trying to _____ .

3 The other night I _____ a man climbing in
through my neighbour's window so I immediately called the
police.

4 Dear Sir,
May we _____ your _____ the
fact that payment of your telephone bill is seriously overdue.

5 If someone told you that you were _____ , would
   you just accept it, or would you take offence?

6 In a race, every second counts, so don't _____
   looking back to see who is behind you.

7 After the bang on the head, I started _____ .
   I could see two of my wife and I didn't know which one to kiss!

8 If Laura gets the job in Florida, it will mean

   _____ .

9 Why are you forever _____ my work? Why can't
   you praise me for once?

10 In the event of rain, the competition will _____
   in the Village Hall.

'Wrap up well, we don't want you to catch cold, do we?'

Take care not to put in an article in these set expressions, e.g. *catch sight
of*, not ~~catch the sight of~~ or ~~catch a sight of~~.

58 Verb and adjective

Match the adjective with its verb. Choose from the three possible answers.

1   They tied King Kong with huge chains, but he still managed to
**break** loose.

    (a)) break   b) turn   c) go

2   Marry me, and I will make all your dreams _____ true.

    a) come   b) grow   c) turn

3   Why is it that so many poets _____ young? Even Byron
only reached the age of thirty-six.

    a) wear   b) fall   c) die

4   Take this medicine and you will soon _____ better.

    a) go   b) get   c) fall

5   I think I'll _____ mad if I have to listen to any more
political speeches!

    a) fall   b) go   c) grow

6   If you find yourself in a field with a bull, _____ still and it
will leave you alone. Probably.

    a) go   b) get   c) stand

7   Please _____ sure your seat belt is fastened for take-off.

    a) make   b) get   c) keep

8   If you _____ quiet, you might be able to hear the grass
growing.

    a) stand   b) fall   c) keep

9   Why does your nose _____ blue when you're cold?

    a) break   b) turn   c) come

10   His excuses for being late are beginning to _____ thin.

    a) wear   b) stand   c) get

59 Almost an alphabet!

Match the verbs on the left with the nouns on the right. Write the answers in the grid below.

1	ask	a	a business, risks, short
2	break	b	a door, a bank account
3	catch	c	a good time, second thoughts, fun
4	do	d	a letter
5	eat	e	a meal, your words
6	fall	f	a question, the way, for the bill
7	go	g	asleep, short
8	have	h	attention, the bill, a compliment
9	infect	i	a window, your promise
10	jump	j	business, your best, someone a good turn
11	keep	k	cold, a ball, a bus
12	lose	l	'no' in the referendum.
13	make	m	lies, the truth, the time
14	name	n	money, love, mistakes
15	open	o	swimming, wrong
16	pay	p	quiet, yourself to yourself, abreast of
17	quit	q	double, the point
18	run	r	a plot, a conspiracy, the truth
19	see	s	your price, the day
20	tell	t	a wound
21	uncover	u	to conclusions, the gun
22	vote	v	touch
23	write	w	your job

We leave x y and z to you!

1	2	3	4	5	6	7	8	9	10	11	12
f											

13	14	15	16	17	18	19	20	21	22	23	

60 Idioms

Replace the words in bold type with an idiom from the box, making any necessary changes.

> beat about the bush   catch sight of   fly off the handle   go dutch
> look on the bright side   mind your own business   pull your leg
> start from scratch   ~~vanish into thin air~~   wear your heart on your sleeve

1   The dog is nowhere to be found.
    He has **completely disappeared**!   *vanished into thin air*

2   When I said your room was a mess,
    I was just **teasing you**.   _____

3   There's no need to **get angry and
    shout** every time the children do
    something wrong.   _____

4   Jack said he would pay for our meal,
    but we said it was much better if we
    each paid for our own.   _____

5   Every time I **get a glimpse** of myself
    in the mirror, I realize I am getting
    older and fatter!   _____

6   Please stop **avoiding the subject**.   _____

7   I had nearly completed the jigsaw
    puzzle when the cat knocked it on the
    floor, so I had to **begin all over again**. _____

8   You can always tell what Tracy is feeling:
    she **can't help showing her emotions**.   _____

9   I know you are upset about the scratches
    on your car, but **think positively**: at least
    they didn't actually steal it.   _____

10 'Why are you all dressed up? Are you
    going out?'
    '**It's got nothing to do with you!**'   _____

Answers

Section 1: Tenses 1

Test 1

A

1 He's riding his bicycle/bike backwards.
2 They are standing on their heads.
3 They are playing guitars/the guitar.
4 He is balancing a broom/brush on his finger.
5 She is eating (the) flowers.
6 He is giving (some) sausages to the dog.

B

1 They deliver letters.
2 They keep the peace/order.
3 They cure people.
4 They sweep (the) roads.
5 They grow fruit and vegetables.
6 They sell meat.

Test 2

1 a are you thinking
   b think
2 a am expecting
   b expect
3 a see
   b is seeing
4 a tastes
   b am tasting
5 a are you having
   b do you have/have you got
6 a am depending
   b depends
7 a imagine
   b are imagining
8 a am weighing
   b do you weigh

Test 3

1 a   2 b   3 c   4 d   5 f   6 e

Test 4

1 was going
2 was doing
3 had
4 was
5 shouted/was shouting (would shout is also possible)
6 managed
7 was performing
8 was waving/waved
9 sank
10 found (had found is also possible)
11 was floating
12 flew
13 looked
14 said
15 did you do (have you done is also possible)

Test 5

1 lived
2 rented
3 had to
4 would come
5 have never seen
6 haven't had
7 have come
8 didn't do (haven't done is also possible)
9 went
10 had just fallen
11 came
12 remembered
13 took
14 waited
15 Didn't you sleep
16 didn't

Test 6

1 have seen
2 looked it up
3 phoned
4 assured
5 went on
6 have been listening
7 have both been misled
8 looked at
9 have ever even seen
10 heard

Test 7

1 dreamt (or dreamed)
2 eaten
3 woke up
4 found
5 given
6 made
7 went
8 sank
9 hung
10 fell
11 felt
12 said
13 lost
14 kept
15 ate
16 ran
17 ate

Test 8

1 travelled
2 arrived
3 had done
4 just smiled/would just smile
5 could
6 were still wearing
7 were sitting
8 happened/has happened
9 had/have had/have been having
10 fell
11 were covered
12 did not reply
13 had been left/was left
14 had not been done/were not done
15 was
16 was watching
17 had spilled (or spilt)
18 was reading
19 come
20 didn't do/haven't done

Test 9

1 h   2 j   3 i   4 d   5 g   6 a   7 c
8 e   9 f   10 b

Test 10

1 e, k   4 c, d
2 b, h   5 a, j
3 f, g, i

Test 11

1 c
I'm practising for the gig. It's
going to be / It's / It will be our
best gig yet!

2 b
It's on Saturday. It starts / It will
start at eight o'clock and goes on /
will go on until Midnight.

3 a
I can't! I'm revising / I'll be
revising for my exams.

4 e
I guess you're right. OK, I'll come
to the concert.

5 d
Thanks, Adrian! That'll save / That
saves me a few quid!

Section 2: Auxiliary verbs

Test 12

A

1 Do you like
2 Did you get
3 Do you study
4 Did you hear
5 Are your students
6 Have the other children read
7 Did you ring
8 Does anyone else need

B

1 I don't like
2 I didn't do/couldn't do
3 he hasn't washed
4 he didn't shake
5 I haven't got/I don't have
6 they don't/can't speak
7 he wasn't listening
8 she doesn't play

Test 13

A

1 b   2 b   3 a   4 a   5 b   6 c   7 b
8 a   9 b